WORST OF THE WORST

SHIPWRECKS!

by Aaron Sautter

CAPSTONE PRESS
a capstone imprint

Published by Capstone Press, an imprint of Capstone
1710 Roe Crest Drive, North Mankato, Minnesota 56003
capstonepub.com

Library of Congress Cataloging-in-Publication Data is available on the Library of Congress website.

ISBN: 9798875244971 (hardcover)
ISBN: 9798875244926 (paperback)
ISBN: 9798875244933 (ebook PDF)

Summary: When disaster strikes at sea, survival is never guaranteed! In this fact-filled nonfiction book, explore history's worst maritime disasters. From shipwrecks lost to the ocean depths to modern ferry disasters, uncover the causes, the impact, and what experts have learned to prevent future tragedies.

Editorial Credits:
Editor: Donald Lemke; Designer: Tracy Davies; Media Researcher: Svetlana Zhurkin; Production Specialist: Whitney Schaefer

Image Credits:
Associated Press: 15, Bullit Marquez, 17, Burt Emanulle, 13; Bridgeman Images: © SZ Photo/Scherl, 25; Getty Images: AFP, 27, artvea (wave icon), spine and throughout, Extreme-Photographer, cover, Karen Kasmauski, 21, lasagnaforone (wave design element), cover and throughout, Manfred Bortoli, 5, Mutlu Kurtbas (bubbles design element), cover and throughout, Natalie Fobes, 19, 20, Ralph White, 9, StanOd, 4, Sygma/Tony Savino, 23; Newscom: ABACA/Eric Vandeville, 29; Shutterstock: Andrea Izzotti, 18, Everett Collection, 8, 10, 11, VVadi4ka (torn paper), cover and throughout; SuperStock: Image Asset Management/World History Archive, 7

Printed and bound in China. PO 6459

TABLE OF CONTENTS

Words in **BOLD** are in the glossary.

INTRODUCTION

DANGEROUS SEAS

FLASH! Lightning fills the sky. *BOOM!* Thunder crashes through the air. *WHOOSH!* Waves smash over a ship's deck. *CRACK!* The ship's **hull** breaks. Soon, the ship sinks, taking everyone with it.

Shipwrecks are terrible disasters. They often cause great damage or take many lives. Prepare to discover some of the worst shipwrecks of all time.

CHAPTER 1

RMS TITANIC

DISASTER STATS

Date: April 14, 1912

Location: North Atlantic Ocean, about 400 miles (644 kilometers) from Newfoundland, Canada

Lives Lost: 1,503

It was a quiet, star-filled night. The ocean was as smooth as glass. But suddenly, a huge iceberg loomed in the dark. The RMS *Titanic* could not turn in time. The iceberg tore several holes in the ship. It quickly filled with water.

Soon, the *Titanic*'s **stern** rose into the air. Passengers fled to the ship's 20 **lifeboats**. But the boats couldn't hold everyone. The ship soon split in half. Then it sank below the icy water. A total of 1,503 people died in history's most famous shipwreck.

The remains of the *Titanic* still rest on the ocean floor.

FACT!

The RMS *Titanic* was the biggest ship ever built at that time. Many people thought it was unsinkable.

CHAPTER 2

RMS *LUSITANIA*

DISASTER STATS

Date: May 7, 1915

Location: Celtic Sea, about 11 miles (18 km) from Ireland's coast

Lives Lost: 1,198

In May 1915, the RMS *Lusitania* was heading to Liverpool, England. It carried 1,959 passengers and crew. But during World War I (1914–1918), German submarines hunted the seas around Britain. At 2:10 p.m., German **torpedoes** hit and sank the *Lusitania*. The disaster took the lives of 1,198 people.

FACT!

At least 128 Americans on the *Lusitania* were killed.

CHAPTER 3

SS EDMUND FITZGERALD

Date: November 10, 1975

Location: Lake Superior, about 17 miles (27 km) from Whitefish Point, Michigan

Lives Lost: 29

The SS *Edmund Fitzgerald* was one of the largest **ore** ships on Lake Superior. But its size couldn't save it. On November 10, 1975, a powerful winter storm hit. Wind gusts blew up to 80 miles (130 km) per hour. People reported waves as high as 35 feet (10.7 meters)!

EDMUND FITZGERALD

By 7:15 p.m., the *Edmund Fitzgerald* disappeared from **radar** screens. Ships later returned to search for it. But they found only two life rafts, some **debris**, and no survivors. The reason for the ship's sinking is still a mystery.

FACT!

Canada declared the wreck of the *Edmund Fitzgerald* to be a protected site. It is illegal to dive or remove items from the site without a license.

Members of the U.S. Coast Guard examine a life raft from the SS *Edmund Fitzgerald* on November 12, 1975.

CHAPTER 4

MV *DOÑA PAZ*

DISASTER STATS

Date: December 20, 1987

Location: Tablas Strait, Philippines

Lives Lost: 4,385

Thousands of people slept on board the MV *Doña Paz*. Most were traveling to Manila, Philippines, for Christmas. But at 10:30 p.m., the ship crashed into an oil tanker ship. The crash caused a huge explosion. Fire spread over both ships and the water. More than 4,300 people were killed.

Family members honor victims of the disaster on January 3, 1988.

FACT!

Only 26 people were rescued after the MV *Doña Paz* disaster.

CHAPTER 5

EXXON VALDEZ

DISASTER STATS

Date: March 24, 1989

Location: Prince William Sound, Alaska

Damage: at least 1,300 miles (2,092 km) of polluted shoreline and countless wildlife killed

A spill-containing barrier surrounds the *Exxon Valdez*.

Alaska's Prince William Sound was a nature-lover's dream. But on March 24, 1989, disaster struck. The oil tanker *Exxon Valdez* ran into a **reef**. More than 11 million gallons (41.6 million liters) of oil spilled into the water.

The Exxon oil company paid billions of dollars for cleanup efforts. But the damage was done. The oil **polluted** most of the area. Thousands of animals died. Some places are still covered in oil to this day.

Workers scrub oil off rocks on the beach of Green Island, Alaska, in 1989.

FACT!

At the time, the *Exxon Valdez* disaster was the biggest oil spill ever in the United States.

CHAPTER 6

NEPTUNE

DISASTER STATS

Date: February 16, 1993

Location: Gulf of Gonâve, Haiti

Lives Lost: 1,500–1,800

On February 16, 1993, the **ferry** *Neptune* was hit by a fierce storm. Frightened passengers rushed to the top deck. But the deck collapsed. Many people were crushed. The ship then **capsized** and sank. Between 1,500 and 1,800 people died in this tragic disaster.

People reacting to the news about their relatives dying on the ferry

FACT!

Only 800 tickets were sold for the *Neptune* when it sank. But survivors said there were at least 2,000 people on the ferry that night.

MV WILHELM GUSTLOFF

Date: January 30, 1945

Location: Baltic Sea, about 19 miles (31 km) from Poland coast

Lives Lost: More than 9,000

On January 30, 1945, World War II (1939–1945) was nearing its end. Germany's MV *Wilhelm Gustloff* was jam-packed with more than 10,000 people. They were fleeing Soviet Union forces. But that night the ship was hit by Soviet torpedoes. People scrambled to get on lifeboats. But most didn't make it. Only 1,239 survived.

FACT!

The MV *Wilhelm Gustloff* was originally a fancy passenger ship. It was built to carry only about 2,000 people.

MV LE JOOLA

DISASTER STATS

Date: September 26, 2002

Location: Atlantic Ocean, near coast of The Gambia

Lives Lost: 1,863

The MV *Le Joola* was carrying about 2,000 people on September 26, 2002. That night, fierce winds and waves capsized the ship. Many people were trapped inside. The *Le Joola* floated upside-down until it sank the next day. More than 1,800 people lost their lives.

FACT!

The *Le Joola* is sometimes called "Africa's *Titanic*."

CHAPTER 9

COSTA CONCORDIA

DISASTER STATS

Date: January 13, 2012

Location: Giglio Island, Italy

Lives Lost: 32

On January 13, 2012, more than 4,000 people were enjoying an Italian **cruise**. But then disaster struck. The *Costa Concordia* hit jagged rocks. The ship soon tipped sideways. It partly sank next to Giglio Island, Italy. Most people were rescued. But 32 were killed.

FACT!

It took almost two and a half years to remove the *Costa Concordia* from where it sank.

GLOSSARY

capsize (KAP-sahyz)—to overturn, or turn bottom up

cruise (KROOZ)—a fun trip in which people travel on board a ship

debris (duh-BREE)—the remains of something that has been broken or destroyed

ferry (FAIR-ee)—a large boat used to carry passengers, vehicles, or cargo over a body of water

hull (HUHL)—the outermost shell or covering of a ship that allows it to float

lifeboat (LAHYF-boht)—a small boat carried on a ship used in an emergency or to help rescue people

ore (OHR)—rocks or minerals that are mined and processed to create metal

pollute (puh-LOOT)—to make foul or unclean

radar (RAY-dahr)—a device that uses radio waves to find the location and distance of an object

reef (REEF)—a ridge made of sand, rocks, or coral found at or near the surface of the water

stern (STURN)—the rear part of a boat or ship

torpedo (tohr-PEE-doh)—an underwater missile used for destroying ships or submarines

READ MORE

Hubbard, Ben. *Lost at Sea! Shipwrecks: The Incredible Stories of the World's Most Famous Shipwrecks.* Dublin, Ireland: Lonely Planet, 2023.

Parkin, Michelle. *Great Lakes Shipwrecks.* Minneapolis: Jump!, Inc., 2024.

Wible-Freels, Korynn. *Shipwrecks: All True and Unbelievable!* Orlando. FL: Ripley Publishing, 2020.

INTERNET SITES

National Geographic Kids: Twenty Top Titanic *Facts*
natgeokids.com/uk/discover/history/general-history/would-you-have-survived-the-titanic

Nautical Channel: The 20 Most Famous and Impactful Shipwrecks in History
nauticalchannel.com/new/shipwrecks

Sky History: Top 10 Most Famous Shipwrecks
history.co.uk/shows/billion-dollar-wreck/top-10-most-famous-shipwrecks

INDEX

ABOUT THE AUTHOR

Aaron Sautter is an author and editor of dozens of cool books for young readers. He enjoys a wide range of subjects from dramatic history and sports to spooky aliens and fantastic creatures. Aaron lives in Minnesota with his wife and two children. In his spare time Aaron enjoys cheering for the Minnesota Vikings and going for long walks with his goofy, lovable dogs.